THE AARON BURR TREASON TRIAL

A Headline Court Case

Headline Court Cases

THE AARON BURR TREASON TRIAL

A Headline Court Case

Eileen Lucas

E⎮⎮ Enslow Publishers, Inc.

40 Industrial Road   PO Box 38
Box 398   Aldershot
Berkeley Heights, NJ 07922 Hants GU12 6BP
USA   UK

http://www.enslow.com

My grateful thanks to Bill Schutte for all his help

Library of Congress Cataloging-in-Publication Data

Lucas, Eileen.
   The Aaron Burr treason trial : a headline court case / Eileen Lucas.
      p. cm. — (Headline court cases)
   Summary: Discusses the treason trial of Aaron Burr, who had served as vice-
president under Jefferson and stood accused of trying to start a war between the United
States and Spain for his own enrichment.
   Includes bibliographical references and index.
   ISBN 0-7660-1765-6 (hardcover)
    1. Burr, Aaron, 1756–1836—Trials, litigation, etc.—Juvenile literature. 2. Trials
(Treason)—United States—Juvenile literature. [1. Burr, Aaron, 1756–1836—Trials,
litigation, etc. 2. Trials (Treason) 3. Vice-Presidents.]   I. Title. II. Series.
   KF223.B8L83 2003
   345.73'0231—dc21
                          2002012520

Printed in the United States of America

10 9 8 7 6 5 4 3 2 1

To Our Readers: We have done our best to make sure that all Internet Addresses in this
book were active and appropriate when we went to press. However, the author and pub-
lisher have no control over and assume no liability for the material available on those
Internet sites or on other Web sites they may link to. Any comments or suggestions can be
sent by e-mail to comments@enslow.com or to the address on the back cover.

Photo Credits: All photos are from the Library of Congress, except as follows:
Courtesy of Blennerhassett Island Historical State Park, pp. 36, 57, 63, 73, 96
(© 1999 by Brian B. Schroeder); Dover Publications, pp. 34, 45, 78; Collection
of the New-York Historical Society, pp. 3, 8, 41, 47, 53, 99; The Virginia
Historical Society, p. 67.

Cover Illustration: Courtesy of Blennerhassett Island Historical State Park.

Contents

chapter one

PRISONER!

FEBRUARY 1807—Late one night in a small village in Mississippi Territory, in what would one day become Alabama, two men on horseback stopped to ask directions to the home of Colonel John Hinson. The man they asked, Nicholas Perkins, pointed the way and then watched as the two riders galloped off. Perkins immediately went for the sheriff, Theodore Brightwell. He informed Brightwell that he believed that one of the horseback riders was none other than former vice president of the United States, Aaron Burr.

Perkins knew that the territorial governor had offered a $2,000 reward for the arrest of Burr. Burr had been accused of trying to start a war between the United States and Spain so that he could lead soldiers into Mexico to obtain power and riches. It was also said that he wanted some of the western states to leave the United States and join with him in creating a new country. Despite the rough clothes and beaver hat Burr had

Aaron Burr, who had been vice president of the United States, was arrested in 1807 and charged with treason.

used to disguise himself, Perkins had noticed that the man wore expensive boots and spoke in an educated manner. But the main thing that gave him away was his eyes—eyes that sparkled like diamonds, as Burr's eyes had been described.

Perkins and Sheriff Brightwell went to Colonel Hinson's place. They saw that the two horseback riders were there. Perkins waited outside in the dark while Brightwell went in. When time passed, Perkins decided to get more help. He went to Fort Stoddart, an outpost near the border between the American-controlled territory of Mississippi and the Spanish-owned Floridas, returning early in the morning with the commanding officer, Lieutenant Edmund Pendleton Gaines, and a party of soldiers. A few miles from Hinson's, they met Burr, who seemed to be trying to escape to Florida. Burr was arrested.

Burr spent several weeks at Fort Stoddart, mostly playing cards with the wife of the commanding officer. But Gaines was afraid that Burr would escape, or worse yet, get some of the local citizens to join him in an attack on the nearby Spanish territory. Gaines arranged for Perkins and a party of soldiers to deliver Burr for trial in the east. This group headed out on March 15 toward the nation's capital, a journey of some fifteen hundred miles through swamps, forests, and wilderness.

By day they traveled single file along narrow trails, some of Burr's guards riding in front of him, some behind. At night, Burr was allowed to sleep in the one small tent they had, while the others camped on the cold, hard ground. Often, the darkness was filled "with the cry of the panther, answered by the howl of the hungry wolf ringing in his ears; while the moaning of the winds through the tops of the lofty trees added dreariness to the solitude."[1]

Perkins had been warned that there might be friends or sympathizers along the way who would try to set Burr free, so he tried to keep away from towns and villages as much as possible. But one day, as they rode through a small town in South Carolina, they passed a tavern where people were gathered outside. Suddenly Burr jumped off his horse and shouted at the townspeople. "I am Aaron Burr," he told them, "under military arrest, and [I] claim the protection of the civil authorities."[2] Immediately Perkins jumped off his horse, grabbed Burr by the waist, and lifted him back on his horse. Another member of the group took the reins of Burr's horse and led him away. Burr, who was reported to have endured all the discomforts and dangers of wilderness travel without complaint, finally broke down and wept in frustration. Some of his captors wept in sympathy.

When the group reached Fredericksburg, Virginia, a message from President Thomas Jefferson instructed them to take the prisoner to Richmond, Virginia, instead of Washington. On the evening of March 26, 1807, Aaron Burr was delivered there to the Eagle Tavern, also known as Mr. Epps's Hotel. There he was released from military custody and turned over to the American justice system.

A New Country

The United States of America was still a very new country in 1807. In 1781, during the Revolutionary War against

Great Britain, American leaders had created the Articles of Confederation to link the newly formed states together. In 1787, delegates from those states wrote the U.S. Constitution, which established a stronger federal government. George Washington, the beloved military leader of the Revolutionary War, became the first president and served two four-year terms. With all the problems America faced as a new country, Washington tried to keep the nation from becoming involved in international conflicts. But the power struggles of Britain, France, and Spain interfered with American business and shipping, sparked conflict along the frontier borders, and threatened to tear the new country apart.

The next two presidents, John Adams and Thomas Jefferson, also faced challenges at home and internationally. One of the problems included Spanish troops along the southern and western borders of the United States in the Spanish possessions of Florida and Louisiana. Because of the difficulty in trying to transport farm produce and other products eastward over the Appalachian Mountains, settlers west of the original thirteen colonies sent their goods to market by way of the Ohio and Mississippi rivers to New Orleans. But New Orleans was controlled by France, and then Spain, and then France again. Sometimes these nations let the Americans use the port of New Orleans, and sometimes they did not. When they did not, it caused serious hardship for western settlers, to the point that many westerners demanded war with Spain. Some threatened to lead troops to New Orleans even if the national government did not declare war, and then, why stop at New Orleans? There was plenty of talk of taking the fight all the way to Mexico City and pushing the Spanish out of North America altogether.

Soon after becoming president in 1801, Jefferson sent diplomats to France to see if that country, led by Napoleon Bonaparte, would guarantee Americans access to the port of New Orleans. If America could purchase New Orleans, it would be even better still. When the French offered to sell all of Louisiana Territory, the Americans were astounded. In April 1803, they agreed to what would become known as the Louisiana Purchase. Now New Orleans and the land along both sides of the Mississippi River would be controlled by the United States. A strip along the southern border of the United States known as West Florida, as well as Texas, the Southwest, and California, was still owned by Spain.

This greatly pleased most Americans living west of the Appalachians but was seen as a threat by some northeastern states. They feared that as western states grew stronger and more populated, eastern states would lose the control of the

The French, under Napoleon Bonaparte, sold the Louisiana Territory to the United States in 1803.

federal government they currently held. Some even thought that some of the New England states should leave the Union and form a separate country.

This was the setting in which the activities of Aaron Burr would take place. Burr was a gentleman, a lawyer, a man who had risen to the rank of colonel in the Revolutionary War and had been elected to the office of vice president of the United States. Exactly what he meant to do in the West remains a matter for debate to this day. Did he want to invade Mexico, free it from the Spanish, and make himself emperor there? Did he plan to include territory that was part of the United States in that empire, or would he merely have welcomed that territory if its citizens chose to join him? Would he have settled happily on his western lands and lived as a U.S. citizen, ready to serve his country in battle against its Spanish neighbor if called upon? There are as many opinions about these questions as there are people who study the records and letters of the time. It depends at least in part on whose side of the story you choose to believe, since the different sides definitely tell different stories. What we do know is that he accomplished none of these things, but he would be branded by many, including Thomas Jefferson, as a traitor to his country.

chapter two

LAWYER AND POLITICIAN

BACKGROUND—Aaron Burr was born in Newark, in the colony of New Jersey, on February 6, 1756. His father, also named Aaron Burr, was a respectable minister and teacher who became president of the College of New Jersey, the school that would later become Princeton University. His mother, Esther Edwards Burr, was the daughter of the great Puritan preacher Jonathan Edwards. Aaron and Esther Burr's first child was a daughter, Sarah, called Sally, born in 1754.

Tragedy came early to this family. While the children were very young, in September 1757, their father died after suffering from a fever. Their grandfather came to Princeton to become president of the college, but he died of smallpox in February 1758. A few weeks later, the children's mother died from the same disease. Their grandmother was going to take care of them, but then she too died. From the time Aaron was two and a half and Sally was not quite five, they were raised in the home of their mother's brother, Timothy Edwards.

Aaron showed a lot of ambition and little patience from childhood onward. Stories say that he ran away from home at the age of four because of a "controversy" with Uncle Timothy and managed to hide for several days before being found. At the age of ten, he tried to run away to sea. His uncle found him clinging to the mast of a ship in the harbor; Aaron would not come down until his uncle agreed to his "peace terms," which included a promise that the boy would not be punished for running away. It seems that Timothy Edwards was very strict when it came to discipline, and the young boy may have found some of his uncle's Puritan ways harsh.

He was very bright and managed to enter the College of New Jersey in 1769 at the age of thirteen—as a sophomore. He was a great reader and did extremely well in his studies. He graduated with honors from college at sixteen, briefly attended a school for ministers, and then switched to the study of law. Slender and somewhat short (about five feet five inches tall), Aaron was considered handsome, polite, and charming. He dressed fashionably and was popular with ladies throughout his life.

When the American War for Independence began, Aaron Burr hurried off to serve. In September 1775, at the age of nineteen, he joined a force that was heading for Canada. During the difficult wilderness trek and the unsuccessful wintertime attack on Quebec in which General Richard Montgomery was killed steps away from him, the young

Aaron Burr achieved a great deal at a young age. After graduating from college at age sixteen, he joined the army and fought in the American Revolution at nineteen, in 1785. By the time he left the army six years later, he had reached the rank of colonel.

Aaron Burr developed leadership qualities that became very much a part of his character. Interestingly, he served under Benedict Arnold, a man whose name, like Burr's, would one day be connected to charges of treason and villainy.

After the Quebec campaign, Burr returned to New England in May 1776. He served briefly on George Washington's staff but preferred to be in a leadership position. He helped guide a retreat after the Battle of Long Island. After wintering with Washington's army near Valley Forge, he participated in the Battle of Monmouth in New Jersey.

Burr's success in the army eventually earned him the rank of colonel, but he found time for other interests as well. He began visiting a lady who lived in Paramus, New Jersey. She was Mrs. Theodosia Prevost, the wife of a British army officer and the mother of five children. She was intelligent and well-read. She was ten years older than Burr, but with his intelligence and ambition, and experience gained in war, he was mature beyond his years. When word came in 1781 that Theodosia's husband had died, probably from a fever, while serving with the British army in Jamaica, Burr began courting her seriously.

By this time, Burr had resigned from the army due to poor health and feelings that his talents were not fully appreciated. He returned to his study of law and became a lawyer in New York State in the spring of 1782. He and Theodosia were married that summer. The war soon ended, and Burr's law practice did very well in New York City. In June 1783, the Burrs' daughter, Theodosia, was born.

During the Revolutionary War, Burr joined in an unsuccessful attack on Quebec. Shown are soldiers moving their boats over Skowhegan Falls during the Quebec campaign.

Federalists and Republicans

In the fall of 1783, Burr began his political career when he was elected to the New York State Assembly. Even though George Washington warned that political parties could turn friends into enemies, many of the politicians of the day were beginning to align themselves into opposing parties. On one hand were the Federalists, who believed in a strong central government. They tended to view the British as important allies for the United States. They were led by a young New York lawyer named Alexander Hamilton.

On the other hand were the Republicans, also known as the Democratic Republicans, or Anti-Federalists, who believed that more power should be kept in the hands of the states and the people. They generally hated the British and preferred to see France as America's best foreign friend. They were represented by Virginian Thomas Jefferson. As Burr began to get involved in politics, he often tried to play the role of compromiser, trying hard to avoid being identified with any one party. He ended up with friends, and enemies, in both groups.

One of Burr's enemies among the Federalists was Alexander Hamilton. As fellow lawyers, the two often met in the courts of law as well as at parties and dinners. On these occasions, they showed their respect for each other's talents and accomplishments, though there were dramatic differences in their political points of view. Both were extremely ambitious, and often a victory for one meant a defeat for the other.

Burr continued to be successful in politics, gaining

attention as attorney general of New York in 1789. In 1791, he was elected to the United States Senate from New York. He defeated General Philip Schuyler, Alexander Hamilton's father-in-law, and this only deepened Hamilton's dislike for Burr. Some people think that from this point on, a major battle between the two was inevitable. When Burr started looking around at other political positions, Hamilton worked hard to keep him from being elected. Still, during his years in the Senate, Burr continued to avoid aligning himself with either party, even to the point of leaving the Senate chamber during highly controversial votes.

A great cause for concern for Burr during this time was his wife's health. For some time, Theodosia had been suffering from a mysterious illness and was increasingly in great pain. Burr repeatedly consulted many of the best doctors of the time to find a cure for her weakness and frailty, and he traveled one hundred miles on horseback from Philadelphia, where the Senate met, to their home in New York, as often as possible. Despite all his care, Theodosia died in May 1794. Their daughter was nearly eleven. Young Theodosia and her father had always been very close, and they grew even closer now as Burr carefully supervised her education. Already Theodosia had read more classic literature than some educated men in the country, and certainly more than was customary for a young girl. Burr saw to it that she learned to speak German and French and could play the harp and pianoforte. Burr's passionate interest in his daughter's education was extremely unusual for his day.

The Elections of 1796 and 1800

In 1796, George Washington refused to accept a third term as president, and the United States had its first election with individuals from different parties. John Adams, who had been Washington's vice president, represented the Federalist point of view. He was opposed by Thomas Jefferson, who had served as secretary of state under Washington. Jefferson was the leader of the Republicans. The Constitution had established the electoral college, which would vote for the president based on electors chosen from each state. When the electoral college met, Adams received the most votes, so he became the next president of the United States. Jefferson had the second-most votes, so he became vice president, even though he and Adams were political opponents representing different parties.

At this time, Burr's Senate term came to an end. He continued to see himself as a military leader, and when it looked as if there might be war with France in 1798, he tried desperately to get a high position in the army. But George Washington, who was once again commander in chief of the army, did not trust Burr. He wrote to President Adams, "From all I have known and heard, Colonel Burr is a brave and able officer, but the question is whether or not he has equal talents for intrigue."[1] Burr's ambitions and plans, it seems, were not always appreciated. So Burr returned to the New York Assembly. He knew that he needed support from one of the parties, so he began to take the side of the Republicans.

Soon it was time for another national election. The

campaign of 1800 would in some ways be a replay of 1796, with President Adams seeking reelection as a Federalist. Also running for the presidency was the vice president, Thomas Jefferson. Jefferson did not really like or trust Aaron Burr, but he asked Burr to run as his vice president. Burr had a lot of connections in New York, a state that would be important in helping Jefferson defeat Adams.

Adams, in turn, wanted Charles Cotesworth Pinckney to be his vice president. The only problem was that the U.S. Constitution said that whoever got the most votes in the electoral college would be president, and whoever came in second would be vice president. The Founding Fathers had not anticipated that the nation's leaders would be split into political parties with opposing points of view. When the electoral college met in December 1800, the results were stunning: Jefferson 73, Burr 73, Adams 65, Pinckney 64, and John Jay 1. This time the top two candidates were not from different parties, but Burr and Jefferson were tied for the presidency of the United States. Some people thought Burr should just step aside and let Jefferson become president, since that is what the Republicans had intended. Others thought that Burr would be a better choice than Jefferson. According to the Constitution, the United States House of Representatives would have to decide who would be the president.

On February 11, 1801, the House of Representatives met to vote for president. They voted once, and Jefferson and Burr were still tied. For seven days they continued voting until, after thirty-five tries, Jefferson finally won by one vote. In 1804, the Twelfth Amendment would change the electoral college procedure to a separate ballot for president and vice president so that this situation would not happen again.

Vice President Burr

And so by the very narrowest of margins, Aaron Burr became vice president of the United States. Unfortunately, if Jefferson did not completely trust him before all this, his suspicions regarding Burr's ambitions were only increased when Burr did not automatically step aside from the presidency. Jefferson shut him out from the workings of the administration and refused to honor his recommendations for political appointments. Only in his role as the head of the Senate did he have a real job to do, and he did that well. But he did nothing to help the president's supporters in the Senate, and he was not considered loyal to the party he was supposed to be representing. So the Federalists did not like him, and now neither did the Republicans.

During February 1801, before Burr's inauguration as vice president, his daughter, Theodosia, was married to Joseph Alston, from a wealthy South Carolina family. In May 1802, Theodosia and her husband had a baby boy named Aaron Burr Alston after the proud grandfather.

Since Burr was not often invited to gatherings at the president's house, during the winter of 1802–1803, he moved into lodgings in Washington that allowed him to entertain on his own. He particularly enjoyed hosting diplomats from other nations, including the Marquis de Casa

Yrujo, Spain's minister to the United States, and Anthony Merry, Britain's minister to the United States. They would both play a role in the ambitious plans he would create for himself.

In 1803 the United States purchased the Louisiana Territory from France, who had recently repurchased it from Spain. There was a great deal of controversy sparked by the addition of this huge piece of land to the United States. Some Federalists were talking about seceding from, or leaving, the Union for fear that they would now have even less influence. The majority of Americans, however, were pleased and excited about the changes that would come with the addition of this vast territory. On December 20, 1803, the French flag was lowered in the Place d'Armes, a public square in New Orleans, and was replaced by the American flag. On hand were William Claiborne, governor of nearby Mississippi Territory, and General James Wilkinson, commanding general of the U.S. Army.

During the spring of 1804, Burr met with General James Wilkinson, with whom he had served during the Revolutionary War. Perhaps the idea for some sort of adventure in the West began to take shape at this time.

Unfortunately for Burr, in sharing his ideas with Wilkinson, he chose as a partner a particularly untrustworthy man. One writer described him as having a "hard-reasoning brain—and no conscience at all."[2] Wilkinson had been involved in the Spanish Conspiracy, a plan by some westerners to develop a closer relationship with Spain and draw away from the United States. At the same time that he held

Thomas Jefferson, leader of the Democratic Republicans, was elected president in 1801 by a very narrow margin. He had little liking or trust for the man chosen to be vice president—Aaron Burr.

very important political and military positions for the United States, Wilkinson was secretly receiving money from Spain for information he supplied to them. He was referred to by the Spanish as Agent 13. It is not clear how much Burr knew about this.

As the end of Burr's vice-presidential term approached, he gave some thought to plans for the future. Jefferson's popularity as president made it likely that he would win reelection, but it was clear that Jefferson would not want Burr as his vice president again. Burr could return to New York and the practice of law and expect to earn a good living, or he could run for another political office. He chose politics, running for the office of governor of New York. That election was held in the spring of 1804. Burr lost, at least in part, it seems, through the efforts of Alexander Hamilton, who had also played an important role in making sure that Burr did not become president in 1800. With George Clinton of New York selected to run for vice president with Jefferson, this meant humiliating defeats for Burr at both the state and national levels, though he still held the office of vice president for a few months more.

A Tragic Duel

To make matters worse, within the next few months, the simmering feud between Burr and Hamilton reached the boiling point when Burr learned of nasty remarks that Hamilton had made about him during the recent elections. Hamilton had compared Burr to Catiline, an ancient character whose schemes had contributed to the downfall of Rome. And apparently Hamilton had even called Burr "despicable."

Burr wrote to Hamilton, asking for an explanation. Hamilton refused to give any. Things escalated to the point where Burr challenged Hamilton to a duel, and Hamilton accepted. Arrangements were made to settle the affair at 7:00 A.M. on July 11, 1804, at Weehawken, New Jersey. Located on the bank of the Hudson River, Weehawken had been the site of a number of duels, including one in which Hamilton's son Philip had been killed three years before.

As the two men faced each other across the dueling grounds and the command to fire was given, two shots rang out, or so it seems. Even the two witnesses could not be sure exactly who fired first, or where they aimed, or if in fact Hamilton fired at all. In the cloud of gun smoke, however, it was immediately clear that Burr was unharmed, but Hamilton was seriously wounded. Hamilton was taken to a home in New York, where he died a terribly painful death the next day.

As the news spread, Americans were horrified. They forgot that Hamilton and his party had become very unpopular in recent years. They remembered only that Hamilton had been like a son to George Washington, had played a huge role in creating the new Constitution, and had helped see the country through its first difficult years. Though other important leaders had killed men in duels, and both the law and the public looked the other way, this time there was an outpouring of outrage. This was different because Hamilton had been so prominent a citizen and because Burr had so many enemies. Burr was charged with murder in New York and New Jersey.

A Western Project

On July 21, Burr quietly left his home in New York with a couple of boxes of clothes and documents. He first visited Navy hero Commodore Thomas Truxton in New Jersey. He then moved on to Philadelphia, Pennsylvania, and stayed with a friend, Charles Biddle. While avoiding the law of New York and New Jersey, Burr, who was still vice president, met in Philadelphia with two Englishmen— Anthony Merry and Charles Williamson. Williamson was a secret service agent for Britain who was also an American citizen, and Merry was the British minister to the United States. Burr talked with them about plans for "western projects" that would require a lot of money and would be aimed against the government of the United States. He hoped the British would be interested in funding such projects.

The plans that Burr described to Merry included taking territory away from the United States to create a new nation. Later, Burr and his supporters would later insist that they just wanted this anti-American diplomat to believe that their plans were to hurt the United States so that the British would help pay for them. Charles Williamson believed that Burr's plans really focused on conquering Mexico. Burr would wait a long time for funding from Britain, but none would come.

Surprisingly—since Burr's plans were mainly directed

Alexander Hamilton's ongoing feud with Aaron Burr ended tragically in 1804, when Burr killed Hamilton (above) in a duel. Burr was charged with murder, and though he was never tried for that crime, his hopes for further political office were dashed.

against Spain—Burr also talked with the Spanish minister to the United States. He hoped to convince him that his plans would hurt the United States enough to make the Spanish want to help. Did Burr really want to hurt the United States, or was this a trick to throw the Spanish suspicions off and get money?

Word that the governor of New York was going to ask the state of Pennsylvania to send him back to New York sent Burr fleeing once again. He traveled to St. Simon, an island off the coast of Georgia, to visit a friend from the Senate. There he was warmly welcomed and entertained and even enjoyed a week-long visit from his daughter and her husband and baby. He also traveled to the coast of Spanish Florida in a canoe to see some of the Spanish territory for himself.

In October he headed to Washington to complete his term as vice president and to consider what he would do next. The duel had ended any chance for political office. Some friends suggested he restart his law career in a new place. He could not go home. There were still murder indictments outstanding in New York and New Jersey, and he had been declared bankrupt in New York. His home had been seized, and all his possessions were being sold to pay his debts. He had only some money borrowed from his son-in-law and the few other possessions he had escaped with. Since the city of Washington was federal territory belonging to no state, he knew that he would not be arrested there at least until his vice presidency ended on March 4, 1805. After that, however, he would have to be very careful.

Burr was not yet finished leaving his mark as vice president of the United States, however. Supreme Court Justice Samuel Chase would be impeached, and Burr would preside over his trial in the U.S. Senate. Chase was a Federalist who had criticized Jefferson and other Republicans. Chase was acquitted because only a simple majority, and not the two-thirds required, voted for conviction. This acquittal helped keep federal judges independent of the executive and legislative branches of government. It is interesting to note that many of the same individuals who participated in the Chase trial would gather again in two short years for another trial in which Burr would have a very different role to play.

The day after Chase's acquittal, March 2, Burr made his farewell to the Senate. He concluded a brief speech by saying,

> May the Almighty bless you and keep you in all that you do together here and separately in your own homes. I ask only that you not forget me, for I, of a certainty, shall always remember, with respect and affection, the years I spent here. [3]

He left the chamber, and the senators stood and applauded him for his hard work there. It is even said that some of the senators wept. Then he headed for Philadelphia, where he met with the British minister, Anthony Merry, still trying to get money. In April 1805, he headed west by way of Pittsburgh.

chapter three

THE FIRST TRIP WEST

INVESTIGATION—If Burr had decided that his future lay in the West, then it would make sense for him to go there and check things out. Like many others, he would travel by way of rivers, the main highways of the times. He wrote to Theodosia, describing the boat that he purchased:

> Properly speaking, [it is] a floating house, sixty feet by fourteen, containing dining room, kitchen with fireplace, and two bedrooms, roofed from stem to stern; steps to go up, and a walk on the top the whole length; glass windows, etc.[1]

By typical riverboat standards of the day, this "ark" was quite luxurious.

One of Burr's first stops was the home of Harman and Margaret Blennerhassett. They were Irish immigrants who had built a beautiful mansion on a long, narrow island in the Ohio River near Marietta, Ohio. Blennerhassett had used the large inheritance he had brought with him to America to contribute to a number of business dealings along the frontier, and now that inheritance was significantly diminished. Burr hoped to convince him to contribute to his plans, dangling a promise of fortunes to be made in front of him.

Then Burr went to Cincinnati, where he would meet with a group of men who were planning to build a canal around the Falls of the Ohio, near Louisville, Kentucky. These included Jonathan Dayton, an old friend and former senator from New Jersey, and Senator John Smith of Ohio. The canal would never be dug, but through the planning of it, Burr would be able to get some sizable loans, which would be a source of funding for him.

Leaving his boat tied up, he began traveling by land. He visited friends in and around Lexington, Kentucky, and then Nashville, Tennessee. Here he was warmly welcomed by General Andrew Jackson, in charge of the Tennessee militia, and his friends, with waving flags and booming cannons. Jackson had made it clear that he hated the "dons," the Spanish masters of the Mexican people, and would love to see them driven from the American continent. Burr, in turn, made no secret of his desire to lead a liberating expedition against the Spanish colonies, stating often that these plans depended on a war breaking out between the United States and Spain. At times he seemed to hint that he had the support of the United States government itself for these plans.

By June 3, Burr left Nashville and returned via the Cumberland River to his waiting ark on the Ohio. At Fort Massac on the Ohio he met with General Wilkinson. At this time Wilkinson was a brigadier general and commanding

Burr's good friend Jonathan Dayton, at one time a senator from New Jersey, was implicated in what was eventually to be called the Burr Conspiracy.

officer of the whole United States Army, most of which, such as it was, was stationed in the West. Wilkinson was also governor of the Upper Louisiana District. It would certainly be helpful to Burr to make use of Wilkinson's connections.

On to New Orleans

Wilkinson and Burr conferred for four days. Then Burr traveled down the Mississippi River on a boat crewed by some of Wilkinson's soldiers. At numerous stops along the way, Burr was entertained by wealthy planters in their lovely homes. Robert Williams, the governor of Mississippi Territory, shook Burr's hand and wished him well with whatever adventures he had planned.

Toward the end of June, Burr arrived in New Orleans. He would stay for three weeks, in which he would be welcomed and honored in private and in public. This busy seaport city included residents from a variety of backgrounds. Among them were the Creoles, or "ancient Louisianians," as these descendants of the early French settlers in this part of America liked to be called. There were also more newly arrived American frontiersmen and merchants, and visitors from other nations. Burr was enchanted by New Orleans, and many of its citizens seemed pleased with him. During his stay in the city, Burr talked with members of a local organization called the Mexican Association or Mexican Society. These Americans gathered information about Mexico that would be useful to someone seeking to overthrow Spanish control. They were heartily in favor of the war with Spain that almost everyone expected would soon erupt.

Upon leaving New Orleans, Burr traveled northeast, mostly by horseback across the Natchez Trace, a path through some four hundred miles of wilderness, to Nashville. He attended a ball in his honor given by Andrew Jackson, and then made stops in Lexington, Frankfort, and Louisville, Kentucky. All these stops were to make friends with people in the West. It is not clear exactly what plans were being hatched during these many visits, but his travels had begun to arouse suspicions. He had spoken to many people about an invasion of Spanish territory. Though he had no soldiers or boats or other supplies, wild stories began to circulate about what would become known as the Burr Conspiracy.

Harman and Margaret Blennerhassett were Irish immigrants. Aaron Burr involved them in his plans with promises of riches to be made.

Suspicions Arise

On the front page of the *Gazette of the United States*, a Philadelphia newspaper, an anonymous article was published on August 2, 1805, with the headline "Queries." It consisted of a series of questions implying a great conspiracy on the part of Burr to cause a revolution in the American West and set up a new country. Burr believed that the Spanish minister to the United States, the Marquis de Casa Yrujo, was responsible for this article. Spain's best chance to stop Burr might well be to ruin his reputation with the American frontiersmen with rumors of treason.

Meanwhile Burr continued his travels, including traveling to St. Louis to meet again with Wilkinson. Here one of Wilkinson's military aides, Major James Bruff, became disturbed by all the rumors he was hearing. It was hard to tell what side anyone was on. He was fully on the side of his country, the United States. But he was not completely sure about his superior officer or that officer's friend, Aaron Burr. He would watch them both. Later, he would relate several private conversations during that summer in which Wilkinson hinted at a "great secret." But because Bruff would not even pretend to be interested in plotting against the United States, he was never fully let in on the plans.

But what exactly were these plans? Burr had probably seen enough evidence of patriotism by this point to realize that most westerners were relatively loyal to the United States. He would also have seen evidence of a great deal of anti-Spanish feeling, and it is likely that his plans centered around capitalizing on that. He told Andrew Jackson that he and Wilkinson settled on a plan to attack Mexico.

As Burr headed east from St. Louis, Wilkinson sent a letter to the secretary of the Navy, indicating that Burr was up to something but claiming not to know what. Already he was laying the groundwork to betray Burr and cover up his own involvement in the plans. Not knowing this, Burr continued to rely on Wilkinson, knowing that his military connections were essential to the plans. Burr returned to Washington in late November.

A Trail of Rumor

All during the spring and summer of 1805, Burr had been moving about, "leaving a trail of rumor."[2] He hinted that he was planning to set up an empire in the West and that those who followed him would make fortunes. He made it seem as though the government in Washington knew of his plans and would not stop him.

Most likely, Burr's plans depended a great deal on how things developed between the United States and Spain and on how the settlers in the West responded. He would seize upon whatever opportunities presented themselves, whether this meant playing a hero's role in a war against Spanish Mexico or in leading a break between the West and the East.

Long after Burr died, some maps were found among his papers that give some clues to his plans. These hand-drawn maps show the mouth of the Mississippi River and the coast of North America from New Orleans to the Mexican city of

Vera Cruz, and extending inland to Mexico City. Historian
Milton Lomask states:

> These maps are silent but eloquent testimony to the scope of
> their author's plans. . . . For "nothing less than the Empire of
> Spain in North America was at stake"—this was the objec-
> tive of the Burr Conspiracy. That it was illegal is obvious,
> but it was not a betrayal of, or separation from, Burr's own
> country. It was not treasonable.[3]

Back in Washington, Burr was low on funds. His plans
would require a lot more than the loans he had been able to
get from the canal scheme. He hoped that by now the British
minister, Anthony Merry, would have received funds from
England for him. He had not.

Burr also needed to find out if there would be a war with
Spain or not. The Louisiana Purchase had helped solve some
of the westerners' problems by giving the United States control of the Mississippi River and New Orleans. But it had
created new international problems because of uncertain
national borders. The Americans claimed that the western
borders of Louisiana reached to the Rio Grande. The
Spanish were certain the territory ended at the Sabine River.
To the east, Spain still claimed to own West Florida, which
stretched from the Mississippi River and the lakes surrounding New Orleans to the boundary between the present-day
states of Alabama and Florida. Americans wanted to believe
that this territory was included in their purchase.

Jefferson argued for the borders the United States
wanted. The Spanish government said the Americans
claimed too much. The French said they did not know who

was right. Jefferson sent his friend James Monroe to Spain to try to negotiate a settlement. This failed. Jefferson was advised by some to declare war against Spain. Others warned that the United States was too weak for war, especially if France came to the aid of Spain.

During the last months of 1805, former vice president Aaron Burr visited President Jefferson. No one knows for sure how much Burr told Jefferson of his plans, but Jefferson seemed to indicate that there would be no war with Spain.

Who Will Join?

During the winter of 1806, Burr approached a number of military leaders about joining his adventure in the West. He talked to General William Eaton, who had gained fame fighting in a minor naval war in the Mediterranean the year before. He also approached Commodore Thomas Truxton, who had been his friend after the Hamilton duel and who had been forced out of the navy by Jefferson. None of the officers he talked to were interested in joining him.

Burr did have some success in his recruiting efforts, however. Comfort Tyler, formerly a member of the New York Assembly, now in financial difficulty, went to work for Burr, purchasing supplies and recruiting others to join. Other associates were Samuel Swartwout, from a family that had long been friends of Burr's, and Dr. Erich Bollman, another friend.

Besides gathering people to his cause, Burr continued his fund-raising efforts. He wrote to Harman Blennerhassett, who was on the lookout for investment opportunities.

Theodosia, Burr's only child, was devoted to her father. She married Joseph Alston in 1801.

Blennerhassett responded that he would be honored to be associated with Burr in any way. Burr would also get a considerable amount of money from his son-in-law.

Burr continued to make contact with the minister from Spain as well. Jonathan Dayton told the marquis, whom Burr had entertained often in the past, of a bold plan to attack the United States government itself in Washington before sailing to New Orleans to set up a new republic. The Spanish minister loved any idea that would lessen the power of the United States, and he gave the conspirators some money.

During the spring of 1806, Burr again visited Jefferson, perhaps hoping for a political appointment and a last chance to change his mind and make a life for himself in the East. By this time Jefferson had received letters from Joseph Hamilton Daveiss, the U.S. attorney in Kentucky, claiming to have information about treasonous plans being hatched by Wilkinson and Burr. But Jefferson trusted Wilkinson and believed that westerners would be loyal to their elected leaders. For the time being, he ignored these letters. Neither did he offer Burr any military or political appointment, however, and so Burr continued with his plans. In April, Burr wrote to both Blennerhassett and Wilkinson, saying that the project was postponed till December.

At some time during this period, Burr purchased a large piece of land (more than 300,000 acres) along the Washita River in Louisiana Territory known as the Bastrop tract. He helped recruit volunteers by offering them a piece of this property. Later, Senator Smith of Ohio would quote Burr as saying:

> If there should be a war between the United States and Spain, I shall head a corps of volunteers and be the first to march into the Mexican provinces. If peace should be proffered . . . , I shall settle my Washita lands, and make society as pleasant as possible.[4]

By late July 1806, Burr was ready to write to Wilkinson confirming preparations for their project. "Our object, my dear friend," the letter says, "is brought to a point so long desired."[5] This letter, or various copies of it, would cause Burr a great deal of trouble. It would be offered as evidence against him when the adventure fell apart.

This letter from Burr (which, in fact, some historians have proposed was not written by Aaron Burr at all, but rather by his friend Jonathan Dayton) was put in code, or cipher, and taken across the country to Wilkinson. It would not be delivered until October, by which time much had happened. The effects of this letter would be seen later.

chapter four

THE BURR WAR

ADVENTURE—In August 1806, Burr headed west for the second time, returning briefly to Blennerhassett Island. At some point, Theodosia, her husband, and their young child also joined the group that was gathering there. The Blennerhassetts believed that Burr was preparing to make himself emperor of Mexico, with Theodosia as his heir. They also believed that, with time, the western part of the United States would choose to break away and join with Burr in the conquered territory. But all of this continued to depend on a legitimate war between the United States and Spain. If that war did not come right away, the adventurers would become settlers on the land Burr had purchased, and there wait patiently, conveniently near the border, until a better time to strike.

Blennerhassett would provide large sums of money now, with the idea that eventually he would be reimbursed by Theodosia's husband, Joseph Alston. The island would be the

Joseph Alston, Burr's son-in-law, brought Theodosia and their son, Aaron, to Blennerhassett Island and supported Burr in his plans.

assembly point for men and supplies, supervised by the Blennerhassetts, while Burr would travel elsewhere. In Marietta they ordered sixteen boats to carry five hundred men and supplies, to be delivered in early December.

The island was a lively place that autumn. Boats came and went as the young men who had joined up arrived and were assigned jobs. There was corn to be roasted in kilns and water bottles to be filled. All the preparations for an adventure in the frontier and settlement of a new land were being made. When John Graham, an investigator for President Jefferson, talked to Blennerhassett, he was told that the reason for all the preparations was the settlement of the Bastrop lands. These young men clearly saw themselves as adventurers much more than soldiers, though rumors continued to fly.

Meanwhile, Burr again visited Andrew Jackson in Nashville, and again a grand ball was given in his honor. After Burr left, however, Jackson was told that Burr's plans included dividing the Union by seizing New Orleans and inviting the western states to join the nation he would form from the conquered Mexico. All this was to be done with the aid of General Wilkinson and the U.S. Army. Jackson disliked Wilkinson and—seemingly for the first time—came to have doubts about Burr. He would support almost any plan aimed against the Spanish, but to the United States, his loyalty was true.

Jackson wrote a quick letter to Governor William Charles Claiborne in New Orleans, naming no names, but warning him of rumors of revolution. He also sent a letter to

While Andrew Jackson (above) supported Aaron Burr at first, he later had doubts about Burr's loyalty to the United States. However, Burr assured Jackson that his aims were not treasonous.

Jefferson, again naming no names, offering the services of the militia he commanded in "the event of insult or aggression . . . on our government and country FROM ANY QUARTER."[1] He then sent a letter to Burr, confronting him with what he had heard. Burr replied immediately. According to Jackson, Burr's letter contained "the most sacred pledges that he had not nor never had any views . . . hostile to the United States."[2]

When Burr visited again, Jackson became convinced once and for all that Burr's plans did not include treasonous activities. Burr also visited in Lexington with Blennerhassett and the Alstons and then rode out to various places, overseeing various aspects of preparations. He seemed to be getting impatient, even as rumors and newspaper stories describing treasonous plans increased.

Neighbors of the Blennerhassetts' in Wood County, Virginia, planned to send the militia to the island to stop whatever was going on there. Margaret Blennerhassett sent the gardener, Peter Taylor, to warn Burr not to come back. Harman Blennerhassett, however, returned to protect his home and family.

Burr Faces a Grand Jury

For some time, Joseph Hamilton Daveiss, district attorney of Kentucky, had been warning Jefferson about Burr. Thinking that Jefferson had not taken him seriously enough, he now went to Judge Henry Innes in Frankfort, Kentucky, asking for a warrant for Burr's arrest, charging that he was preparing a military expedition against Mexico. When Burr heard about the charges, he wrote to Judge Innes, informing him that he was riding to Frankfort to answer them. He was accompanied by Henry Clay, a young and talented Kentucky lawyer who had recently been appointed to the U.S. Senate and who would one day become a famous statesman. A grand jury then met to consider the charges. It would be their job to see if there was enough evidence to formally indict Burr.

The town of Frankfort in the young state of Kentucky had never seen anything like this before—the former vice president facing a grand jury. A large and loud crowd gathered in the courtroom and overflowed into the hallways and out the doors. During the investigation, two writers for the *Western World*, a newspaper that had written highly exaggerated accounts of Burr's plans, conceded that their reports were based on rumors. The grand jury not only threw out the charge but "signed a written declaration expressing their belief that Burr meditated nothing dangerous to the peace and well-being of the United States."[3] The crowd cheered and then adjourned to a great ball given that night in honor of Aaron Burr. It would be one of the last times that Burr would be the center of so much public affection.

A Disputed Border

About a year earlier, in October 1805, a Spanish force of over a thousand men had crossed the Sabine River along the border between Spanish-owned Texas and American-owned Louisiana. This area was claimed by both nations, and these actions by the Spanish had been part of the reason for all the talk about going to war to settle the matter. After this Spanish "invasion," Major Moses Porter, American commander at Natchitoches, along the Red River in American-claimed territory, sent troops to drive the Spanish back to the western side of the Sabine. But Spanish officials in Texas continued to claim the eastern shores of the Sabine for Spain.

By late spring 1806, General Wilkinson had been instructed to leave St. Louis and descend the Mississippi to defend Americans and American territory from the Spanish. Wilkinson's orders were to move with as much speed as possible, but he did not arrive in Natchez (along the Mississippi River above New Orleans) until September 1806. By that time, Spanish soldiers had again crossed the Sabine and moved eastward toward the American post at Natchitoches. The people of the Mississippi and Orleans (now Louisiana) Territories were expecting at any moment that there would be war, and there was a great sense of excitement in the air. A New Orleans newspaper proclaimed, "We are happy to learn that the Government has at length issued positive orders to repel the aggressions of our enemies by force."[4] This article expressed the hope that when the enemy was pushed back from the border, the war would not end until the people of Mexico were freed from the Spanish.

But Wilkinson continued to move slowly. He took two weeks to get to Natchitoches, a journey that could easily be made in three or four days. When he finally got there, he did send word to the Spanish that they must return to the western side of the Sabine. At first they refused, but then

Henry Clay, who was later to become a famous orator and statesman, rode with Burr to Frankfort, Kentucky, to appear before the grand jury.

suddenly, on September 27, they did retreat, ending the likelihood of conflict.

Wilkinson's Betrayal

General Wilkinson was still at Natchitoches on October 8 when Samuel Swartwout arrived with the coded letter Burr had sent in July. Wilkinson was aware of the rumors going around about a Burr conspiracy, and he wanted to take no chances of having his own part in the plans discovered. He decided to play the role of patriotic citizen and dutiful soldier. After decoding Burr's letter, Wilkinson made a copy with several changes to hide his own involvement in the plans. He would later claim to be unable to find either the first letter delivered by Swartwout or the duplicate delivered a few days later by another friend of Burr's, Erich Bollman.

Wilkinson then prepared a letter to Jefferson, warning of an armed expedition heading toward Mexico but claiming not to know who was leading it. He also sent a messenger to Mexico, asking the Spanish to pay him for saving them from Burr. He sent the bill for this messenger's expenses to Washington, asking the United States to pay for his efforts to betray it to Spain. Because Jefferson trusted Wilkinson, he would agree to pay this bill.

The Sabine crisis ended when the Spanish agreed to a proposal from Wilkinson to respect the territory in question as "neutral ground." Wilkinson made it look like the Spanish were giving up claims to territory, but actually, the Americans were too.

Then Wilkinson prepared to defend New Orleans against the terrible army he seemed to imagine heading there. Burr biographer James Parton reports that "terrible and ridiculous was the excitement he created."[5] Wilkinson wrote a long report to Jefferson, stating dramatically:

> I shall glory to give my life to the service of my country; for I verily believe such an event is probable; because should seven thousand men descend from the Ohio . . . with my handful of veterans, however gallant, it is improbable I shall be able to withstand such a disparity of numbers.[6]

This report would not reach Jefferson until January 1, 1807. But in November, the coded letter from Burr—as altered by Wilkinson—arrived in Washington.

Jefferson's Proclamation

Though Jefferson had done nothing to stop Burr in the face of newspaper articles and letters from citizens alleging sinister plots for well over a year, he now decided to act decisively to end the Burr expedition. On November 27, Jefferson issued a proclamation warning the nation that some persons were conspiring to attack "the dominions of

General James Wilkinson had served with Burr in the Revolutionary War. He proved to be an untrustworthy partner in Burr's scheme for the West; his betrayal led to Burr's downfall.

Spain" and were "deceiving and seducing honest and well-meaning citizens" into joining them.[7]

The proclamation did not mention Aaron Burr by name, but because of all the rumors that surrounded his activities, many Americans decided that Aaron Burr was a traitor. An excitement bordering on hysteria swept the country. It seems that many people assumed that President Jefferson would not have made such a statement unless he had strong proof. In an editorial, the *Lexington Gazette* declared that while they had previously believed that Burr's plans were only for an attack on Mexico in the event of a war with Spain, they had now changed their opinion due to the president's proclamation. Author Walter McCaleb declares:

> The people were caught in the torrent of rumors and swept farther from their moorings than at any other period in the history of America. From east to west, from north to south the country rose from disquietude to panic; and under the influence of the Proclamation from doubt to certainty of the blackness of Burr's designs![8]

There were all kinds of rumors that included troops ranging from two thousand to more than ten times that number. In Wood County, Virginia, there were false reports that Andrew Jackson was raising a thousand men for Burr and that another thousand were coming from Kentucky, Pittsburgh, and elsewhere.[9]

Ohio lawmakers authorized the governor to call out the militia. On December 6, 1806, three hundred militiamen took up positions along the Ohio under orders to stop the fleet if it tried to move down the river. The boats that were being built in Marietta and that were to be delivered to Blennerhassett Island were seized. Hundreds of barrels of food and other supplies that had been ordered by Blennerhassett were also taken.

Trouble on Blennerhassett's Island

With word that the Wood County militia planned to attack the island, those on the island decided to move out. All day on December 10, supplies were carried from the house to several boats that arrived with a group of Burr's recruits. Work continued by lantern light when evening came. Blennerhassett and the recruits pushed off about an hour after midnight.

When the Wood County militia arrived on the island in the morning, they found the place empty except for Margaret Blennerhassett and her children and a few servants. The militia chief, Hugh Phelps, and a few of his men attempted to catch the fleeing boats at a point a few miles downriver. While keeping watch along the shore in the cold, dark night, the militiamen drank so much whiskey that they fell sound asleep. A few hours later, they were unaware that Blennerhassett and company were floating silently by.

Meanwhile, back on Blennerhassett Island, the rest of the militiamen proceeded to make a huge mess out of the house and grounds and to get drunk in the Blennerhassetts' wine cellar. One man, perhaps accidentally, perhaps not, fired his rifle into the entrance hall ceiling. Margaret Blennerhassett and her sons were sitting in the room above that hall but fortunately were unhurt. About a week later,

Margaret Blennerhassett left the island with a small group of adventurers who would take her to join her husband. She took just a few of her husband's books and other possessions with her, with no way to know that she would never see the island or her beautiful home again.

When Burr met up with Blennerhassett on the Ohio on December 27, he learned about the flight from the island ahead of the militia and that many of his boats had been confiscated. Perhaps he should have given up at that point. But he still had the Bastrop lands to settle, and he forged on, reassuring his recruits that he still believed that their adventure would be successful.

On December 29, the group of flatboats rested a mile below Fort Massac, very near to where the Ohio joins the Mississippi. Captain Daniel Bissell, commanding there, visited Burr. Bissell later reported that he saw only "about ten boats of different descriptions, navigated with about six men each, having nothing on board" aside from what settlers would be expected to carry.[10] By the first of the year, they were on the Mississippi.

On January 16, 1807, John Randolph, a member of the House of Representatives from Virginia, and a cousin of Thomas Jefferson, demanded that President Jefferson provide Congress with facts. On January 22, Jefferson sent a variety of documents to Congress, including Wilkinson's translation of Burr's letter, which came to be known as the cipher letter. He also sent a lengthy message dealing with the conspiracy. For the first time, he identified the main objective of that movement as an attempt to divide the nation and named Burr as its leader. He admitted his information was "chiefly in the form of letters, often containing such a mixture of rumors, conjectures, and suspicions, as renders it difficult to sift out the real facts."[11] Under these circumstances, he asserted, "neither safety nor justice will permit the exposing [of] names, except that of the principal actor, whose guilt is placed beyond question."[12]

He then went on to announce that the "prime mover" he referred to was Aaron Burr. Without benefit of a trial and even while admitting that much of his information was rumor, Jefferson declared Burr guilty of a terrible crime. This was wrong, constitutionally wrong, and Jefferson had to have known it. Former president John Adams, while he

Blennerhassett Mansion, on an island in the Ohio River, was the site of Burr's plans for his adventure in the western territories and Mexico.

did not much care for Burr, knew from experience what it was like to be the victim of rumors and slander. Alexander Hamilton had written that Adams was "excessively vain and jealous."[13] Other colleagues had also criticized him and called him names. In a letter to a friend, Adams wrote, "Politicians have no more regard for the Truth than the Devil [and] I suspect that this Lying Spirit has been at Work concerning Burr."[14]

Burr's Friends on Trial

In the meantime, Wilkinson had been busy preparing New Orleans for attack. He arrested anyone who got in his way or dared to disagree with him about the danger ahead. Swartwout and Bollman, carriers of Burr's letters, were arrested, denied legal representation, and sent under military guard to Washington.

Writs of habeas corpus—documents that prevent the government from holding prisoners without sufficient reason—had been ignored. It would seem that the U.S. Constitution—which guarantees the right to a trial in the area where an individual is accused of committing a crime, the right to legal representation, and the right of habeas corpus—had been violated. Soon after the prisoners arrived in Washington, Erich Bollman was taken to Thomas Jefferson for questioning. Bollman told the president that Burr's sole goal was an attack on the Spanish dominions and not a separation of the Union. Jefferson promised that Bollman's words would not be used against him and that the paper on which they were written would not be shared, but he did not honor that promise. During Burr's trial Jefferson would use this document.

The case of *United States* v. *Swartwout-Bollman* was heard in February before the Supreme Court of the United States. Chief Justice John Marshall's opinion in this case would rest on the definition of treason. America's Founding Fathers had wrestled with a definition of treason. After all, they had been guilty of levying war against their king and government when they fought the revolution that freed the colonies. Fortunately for them, they won. Otherwise, many of them would have been tried for treason.

As they established the new country, they needed fair and just laws that would protect the citizens under the new government from tyranny, the kind of power they had fought against. They were especially concerned about the practice in too many countries of the use of the charge of treason to punish anyone who disagreed with the government. This practice of "building up" reasons for this serious crime is known as constructive treason, and it is easy to see how it could be abused by powerful governments. Thus American leaders were very precise when they defined treason in Article III, Section 3 of the Constitution. Treason against the United States consists "only in levying war against them, or in adhering to their Enemies, giving them aid and comfort." Even though conspiring, or planning, to overthrow the government is wrong, it is not treason, according to the Constitution. They said there was a difference between planning a war and actually carrying out that plan. There was no evidence to hold Bollman or Swartwout on a charge of levying war against anyone. They were both set free.

Unfortunately for Aaron Burr, Marshall added an incidental comment about treason that would come into play in Burr's trial:

> It is not the intention of the court to say that no individual can be guilty of [levying war] . . . who has not appeared in arms against his country. On the contrary, if war be actually levied, that is, if a body of men be actually assembled for the purpose of effecting by force a treasonable purpose, all those who perform any part, however minute, or however remote from the scene of action, and who are actually leagued in the general conspiracy, are to be considered as traitors. But there must be an actual assembling of men for the treasonable purpose to constitute a levying of war.[15]

In other words, once an act of war occurred, people who were involved at a distance are guilty as well as those who participate directly. But for this principle to hold true, there has to be an act of war, and in the case of *Swartwout-Bollman* there was not.

A Second Grand Jury

In January 1807, Burr and his group of adventurers tied up at the mouth of a small tributary

This is part of the cipher key used in the letter Wilkinson claimed to have received from Burr. It played an important role in Burr's trial, and Wilkinson admitted to having made changes in the letter.

of the Mississippi north of Natchez called Bayou Pierre. Burr spent the night at the home of Peter Bryan Bruin, a judge of the territorial supreme court. In a newspaper, Burr read that Wilkinson's altered version of the cipher letter had been sent to the president. It was bad enough for Burr's plans that the general had made a deal with the Spanish. Now it was clear what he had probably already suspected: that his old friend had betrayed him. Burr declared that the world would pronounce Wilkinson a villain for his lies. Burr wrote a public letter in which he declared that he would be happy to explain to anyone's satisfaction that his plans were within the law.

Burr's camp on the Mississippi was searched several times by the authorities, but nothing relating to a military expedition could be found. On January 15, at a house near Cole's Creek, Mississippi Territory, Burr met with the acting governor of the territory, Cowles Mead, who promised Burr and his followers the full protection of the law. Burr was then escorted to the little town of Washington (near Natchez), the capital of the territory. Bail was set, and Burr was scheduled to appear before a grand jury under Judge Thomas Rodney in the territorial supreme court on February 2. So many people gathered to see the sight that the little town of Washington was without a room big enough to hold the trial. Despite bone-chilling temperatures, the hearing took place outside, under several large trees that would become known in the town as the Burr oaks.

Wilkinson and Claiborne wrote to Mead, suggesting that

he place Burr on board a military ship and send him to New Orleans. Fortunately for Burr, Mead ignored this suggestion.

Judge Rodney was not exactly friendly toward Burr, however. In his charge to the jury, he said:

> This once illustrious Citizen, has been lately accused of [attempting] to Separate the Western Country of the United States from the Union, and to combine it with . . . Mexico, and to erect them into a New and Independent Empire for himself Or for Some Rich Patron under whom he acts. This accusation has Traversed the United States through the medium of the Press and other channels of communication, has agitated the People, and alarmed The Government in such a Manner as to put them to a great deal of trouble and expense. It will be with you gentlemen to Enquire into the truth of this accusation.[16]

The grand jury listened to the testimony of witnesses and responded on February 4 with a protest against the authorities. "The grand jury of the Mississippi Territory, on due investigation of the evidence brought before them," they reported, "are of opinion that Aaron Burr has not been guilty of any crime or misdemeanor against the laws of the United States, or of this Territory: or given any just cause of alarm or inquietude to the good people of [this territory]."[17] They added that the military expedition that had been raised to arrest him had been unnecessary, since Burr had never put up any resistance to civilian authority.

But the judge claimed that Burr was still required to appear before the court whenever it requested. There were rumors that a military patrol was coming up the Mississippi with orders to turn Burr over to Wilkinson and the military

Burr speaks with his followers. Burr talked openly about his desire to invade Spanish territory and liberate people from Spanish rule.

authorities. There were also rumors that Wilkinson had hired assassins to kill Burr.

It was clear to Burr that his very life was in danger and there would be no justice here. He decided to go into hiding. On February 6 (Burr's birthday), Governor Williams declared Burr a fugitive from justice and offered a $2,000 reward for his arrest.

Burr came out of hiding long enough to pay a secret visit to his followers. He told those who wanted to that they were free to go on to the Bastrop lands and settle there. He suggested they sell the boats and supplies and divide the money among themselves. Then he rode into the wilderness of

Mississippi Territory on a borrowed horse, accompanied by a young guide, Major Robert Ashley.

Blennerhassett began to journey home, but he was arrested in Kentucky after Burr's arrest in Mississippi. Like Burr, he would go on trial for treason in Richmond, Virginia. Many of the rest of the band of adventurers stayed in the territory, eventually becoming "school masters, singing masters, dancing masters, clerks, tavern keepers, and doctors."[18]

chapter five

THE TRIAL

VIRGINIA, 1807—In those days, the justices of the Supreme Court were required to preside over circuit courts as well as the Supreme Court. John Marshall, Chief Justice of the Supreme Court, was assigned to the southern circuit, which included Virginia. Marshall, only a year older than Burr, was described as having eyes as brilliant as Burr's. According to historian James Parton, "It was often remarked during the trial that two such pairs of eyes had never looked into one another before."[1]

Burr was being tried in Virginia's circuit court because the only place anything even remotely close to war—or the "overt act" required by the U.S. Constitution—had occurred was on Blennerhassett Island, and that belonged at the time to Virginia. (It is now part of the state of West Virginia.)

Unfortunately for the prosecution, Burr had not been on the island when the "troops" were assembled there in December 1806, but Chief Justice Marshall himself, in the *Swartwout-Bollman* case, had given the opinion that if a treasonable act had occurred, a conspirator's physical presence was not necessary. So even though grand juries in Kentucky and Mississippi Territory had not seen fit to indict Burr, Virginia would now take a shot at it. The problem with this, as far as the prosecution was concerned, was that this meant the judge for the case would be Chief Justice John Marshall, a man everyone knew to be no friend of President Jefferson.

A Decision on Charges

On March 30, 1807, Burr was turned over to the court by the military guard that had brought him to Richmond. Marshall met with Burr and lawyers from both sides to discuss the charges. The prosecution claimed that there was cause to try him for treason (for gathering an armed force to attack New Orleans) and misdemeanor (for gathering an armed force to attack Spanish territory, a violation of the Neutrality Act of 1794). Burr's bail was set at $5,000. He was to appear the following day in the courtroom of the state capitol, where the discussion would continue on what the charges against him would be.

That courtroom, however, was not nearly big enough for the crowd that wanted to attend. People had come from all over to see if the former vice president was to be put on trial for treason. The case would therefore be heard in the largest room available, which was in the Virginia capitol building. Even there, the crowd still spilled out the doorways. There

The military guard brought Burr to Richmond, the capital of Virginia, for his trial on charges of treason. People came from miles around to attend the trial. Above is the Virginia capitol, shown in an 1831 engraving.

were sand-filled boxes scattered among the benches and chairs in which tobacco juice could be spit in the dingy and dirty room. During the long summer days in which the trial would take place, it would be a hot, uncomfortable setting.

The documents that record the speeches of the lawyers during the months that followed fill many hundreds of pages. Some of these speeches are considered great works of legal argument. But many, many hours were filled with boringly repetitive words, and there must have been days when it seemed that the lawyers were speaking only to themselves.

First, arguments would be heard to the charges against

Burr. Opening for the prosecution, Virginia District Attorney George Hay cited the cipher letter and the affidavits of Wilkinson and Eaton as adequate grounds for suspecting that the former vice president had committed treason by "assemblying an armed force, with design to seize the city of New Orleans, . . . revolutionize the territory attached to it, . . . and separate the western from the Atlantic states," and that he had committed "a high misdemeanor, in setting on foot within the United States, a military expedition against the dominions of the king of Spain."[2]

Two lawyers spoke for Burr, and then he spoke for himself. Burr pointed out that he had already appeared in several courts and been acquitted. His travel on the Ohio and Mississippi rivers had been peaceful, and he had openly discussed his plans in public. He said that he had fled only when he feared an unlawful military arrest would put his life in danger.

Once More, a Grand Jury

Justice Marshall ruled that at this point Burr would be charged only with the misdemeanor. He added that though the prosecution had had plenty of time to gather evidence to prove that an "overt act" had occurred, they had failed to do so. When Jefferson learned of this, he responded angrily that the nation would judge Marshall if he failed to judge Burr appropriately.

Since Burr was to be charged with misdemeanor only, this meant that he could be released from custody if his bail was paid. Marshall set bail at $10,000, and Burr was temporarily free to get ready to face a grand jury, whose job would be to decide if there was enough evidence to indict him (formally put him on trial). When someone is accused of a major crime, the Constitution requires that they be indicted by a grand jury, indicating that there is enough evidence to proceed, before they are put on trial.

The government worked hard to find witnesses who would testify about Burr's activities. Pamphlets were sent out throughout the states and territories, inviting citizens to come forward with information.

Meanwhile, Burr put together a defense team, collected witnesses, and prepared a defense strategy. Burr's panel of attorneys would include Virginians John Wickham, Edmund Randolph, and Benjamin Botts, and Luther Martin of Maryland. Luther Martin had been a member of the Constitutional Convention and had spoken out against slavery. He had since made no secret of his strong dislike for Jefferson and repeatedly claimed that the trial was a case of Jefferson persecuting Burr. Jefferson, in turn, would later call Martin an "impudent Federal bull-dog,"[3] and suggested that Martin should be put on trial as an accomplice to Burr.

But it was Burr himself who would lead his defense team, and he was highly qualified to do so. He appeared neat, dignified, and confident in the courtroom, a place in which he felt at home. He stated that

> months before, a high authority had branded him a traitor, but at this late date, the government was not yet ready to prove it. Even longer ago, the same authority had proclaimed the existence in the West of a civil war. Now

it appeared that the government was unable to locate the conflict. "For six months," said Burr, "have they been hunting for it, and still can not find one spot where it existed. There was, to be sure, a most terrible war in the newspapers; but no where else."[4]

U.S. District Attorney George Hay led the prosecution, though he carefully followed directions he received in numerous letters from President Jefferson during the trial. Jefferson had made it clear that he believed Burr to be guilty. He gave Hay blank pardons to be given to anyone who had had a part in the adventure who would otherwise not testify against Burr, and he repeatedly ignored warnings that his trust in Wilkinson was misplaced.

Also on Hay's team were Virginia attorneys Alexander MacRae and William Wirt. Wirt was known as a great speaker for whom the courtroom audience would sit at silent attention. The judges would be John Marshall and Cyrus Griffin, judge of the District of Virginia.

Thousands came to Richmond from north, south, and west to see the spectacle of the trial. A young writer named Washington Irving, who would one day become famous as the author of the tales of Rip Van Winkle and Ichabod Crane, was among the reporters. He noted Burr's popularity with the women: "Not a lady, I believe, in Richmond, whatever may be her husband's sentiments, would but rejoice in seeing Colonel Burr at liberty."[5]

A young attorney, Winfield Scott, was also there to observe. No one present at the trial could know that forty years later he would lead U.S. troops into Mexico and be called a hero. Burr's friend, Andrew Jackson, was also there. A story is told that Jackson stood on the steps of a store in Richmond one day shouting that Burr was innocent and the president was wrong to persecute him.

So great was the excitement surrounding the trial that when it came time to select members of the grand jury, it was virtually impossible to find anyone who had not made up his mind about the case. John Randolph, a congressman who often argued with Jefferson, admitted to having already formed an opinion in the case, but was chosen for the jury and named foreman.

A Historic Subpoena

On June 9, while the grand jury was still waiting for Wilkinson to appear, Burr made a highly controversial

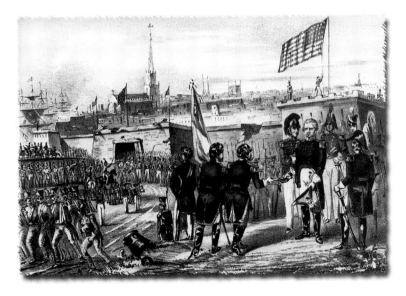

Winfield Scott, one of the observers at Burr's trial, was later to lead the troops that annexed Texas during the Mexican War, in 1847.

move. He asked that President Jefferson be served with a subpoena, requiring him to produce certain documents. The most important of these was the cipher letter supposedly sent by Burr to Wilkinson, an altered copy of which Wilkinson had sent to Jefferson. Burr knew that by establishing doubts about the authenticity of this letter, he could cast suspicion on the government's case. In order to challenge this document, however, it had to be produced.

Could the court issue a subpoena to the president? This had not been done before. If it could, Jefferson feared, it would show that the court was more powerful than the president. Burr's attorneys argued, however, that Burr's right to see the evidence against him was constitutionally protected, and not even the president could deny him that. In what would become a famous speech, Luther Martin argued for Burr:

> The president has undertaken to prejudge my client by declaring that "of his guilt there can be no doubt." He has assumed to himself the knowledge of the Supreme Being himself, and pretended to search the heart of my highly respected friend. He has proclaimed him a traitor in the face of the country which has rewarded him. He has let slip the dogs of war, the hell hounds of persecution, to hunt down my friend. And would this President of the United States, who has raised all this absurd clamor, pretend to keep back the papers which were wanted for this trial, where life itself is at stake?[6]

After listening to long-winded and sometimes highly emotional arguments from both sides, Marshall was ready to decide. On June 13 he responded that the president could not

An able lawyer, Burr led the defense team himself. The defense's subpoena of documents from President Jefferson was a bold step that would set precedent for the next century.

deny an individual's constitutional right to see evidence against him, and a subpoena could be issued.

The Constitution guarantees the right to a speedy and public trial with the accused having the right to gather evidence in his defense. The Constitution does not exempt anyone from this process. It was on the basis of the information contained in the document rather than the position of the person who held it that the court could require it as evidence. In other words, the president is not above the law.

Jefferson sent some of the papers in question to Hay, representing the prosecution. In frustration, however, the president continued to stress that the three branches of government are independent and asked what would happen to the country if the courts "could . . . keep him constantly trudging from north to south and east to west, and withdraw him entirely from his Constitutional duties?"[7]

Wilkinson Testifies

Finally, on June 15, General Wilkinson arrived in Richmond, dressed in full uniform, covered with medals, and expecting to be the center of attention. With him were General William Eaton, an officer to whom the government suddenly paid a large overdue debt when he agreed to testify against Burr, and Sergeant Jacob Dunbaugh, who had been with Burr as he traveled on the Mississippi and who received a promotion when he agreed to testify for the prosecution.

There are two different versions of what happened when Burr and Wilkinson first saw each other in the courtroom. According to a letter that Wilkinson wrote to Jefferson, Burr was too cowardly to look him in the eye. Wilkinson wrote that when his

> eyes darted a flash of indignation at the little traitor, on whom they continued fixed until I was called to the Book . . . this lion-hearted, eagle-eyed Hero, jerking under the weight of conscious guilt, with haggard eyes . . . averted his face, [and] grew pale.[8]

However, the young New England writer Washington Irving described the moment differently. He said that at the mention of Wilkinson's name,

> Burr turned his head, looked him full in the face with one of his piercing regards, swept his eye over his whole person . . . and went on conversing with his counsel as tranquilly as ever.[9]

Wilkinson was kept on the stand for four days in which he stumbled over his words and was forced to admit that he had made numerous changes to the cipher letter. The jury could see that the letter Wilkinson claimed to have received from Burr had been heavily edited to disguise Wilkinson's part in the plans. Thus the letter could not be seriously considered as evidence against Burr. In fact, several members of the jury wanted to indict Wilkinson as a conspirator. Jury foreman Randolph stated, "Wilkinson is the only man that I ever saw who was from the bark to the very core a villain."[10]

Burr Is Indicted

On June 24, the grand jury began to report its findings. Burr and Blennerhassett were indicted for both treason and misdemeanor, even though Marshall had had them committed on the misdemeanor charge only. Five of Burr's associates—Jonathan Dayton, John Smith, Comfort Tyler, Israel Smith, and Davis Floyd—were also indicted on the same charges. Perhaps the grand jury was influenced by the fact that in recent days the U.S. ship *Chesapeake* had been attacked by a British ship, which inspired great patriotism among Americans and a desire to punish anything anti-American. Upon hearing the indictment, Burr stood in the courtroom and said, "I plead *not guilty*, and put myself upon my country for trial."[11]

Now that he had been indicted for treason, Burr could no longer be free on bond. He was moved to the Richmond jail,

The grand jury indictment of Burr and five others may have been influenced by the fact that the USS Chesapeake *(on left) had recently been attacked by a British ship, which aroused a great deal of patriotic fervor.*

a notably filthy place with nowhere for the defense to meet and plan. He was moved to a house rented by Luther Martin, then to the newly built state penitentiary which offered upper-floor apartments that were quite pleasant. A description of Burr's time there would relate:

> Servants were continually arriving with messages, notes, and inquiries, bringing oranges, lemons, pineapples, raspberries, apricots, cream, butter, ice and other articles— presents from the ladies of the city.[12]

Later Burr was moved back to Luther Martin's house.

Just before the trial started, Theodosia arrived with her husband and child. They found the city of Richmond bustling with the crowds that had come for the trial. Once again the court met in the Virginia House of Delegates, and once again it was filled to overflowing.

The Trial Begins

August 3 was the opening day of the trial, and George Hay, the leading attorney for the prosecution, had to admit that he was not ready. He needed more time to prepare his extensive list of witnesses. He was given four days, then three more. By now Burr had been moved into Luther Martin's house, and Blennerhassett had taken his place in the state prison. He had been arrested in Kentucky and brought to Richmond. Once there, he wrote to his wife that he had been assured that "the prosecutions for treason have already become ridiculous among the best informed, so that none of us will probably be hanged."[13] Actually, at that point, the outcome was still uncertain.

Luther Martin, who had been a member of the Constitutional Convention, was one of Burr's defense attorneys. Martin argued that President Jefferson's office should not protect him from having to supply documents in the case.

As with the grand jury, selecting a fair and impartial jury for the trial turned out to be nearly impossible. Everyone had heard about the trial and what the papers had to say about the conspiracy, and many had strong opinions about it. The first forty-eight candidates provided only four suitable jurors. When the next forty-eight candidates were gathered, not one could be found who had a favorable opinion of Burr. Finally, Burr offered to allow the remaining eight positions to be filled without argument, realizing that his job and that of his lawyers was to prove that the case against him was flawed. If they could do that, it would not matter who was on the jury. The defense's main point was that Burr had been hundreds of miles away from Blennerhassett Island on December 10, 1806. Even if he had intended to go to war, he had not levied it. He hoped that this would keep him outside the Constitutional definition of treason.

It was clear from the outset that the trial would hinge on the interpretation of the clauses in the Constitution that say, "Treason against the United States shall consist only in levying war against them," and "That no person shall be convicted of treason unless on the testimony of two witnesses to the same overt act, or on confession in open court."[14]

This was the situation when George Hay opened for the prosecution on Monday, August 17. He admitted that Burr had not been on Blennerhassett Island on December 10, 1806, when the alleged "overt act" occurred, when armed men had supposedly gathered to wage war against the United States. It did not matter, said Hay, since Chief Justice

Marshall himself had said that a man may levy war against his country without being present. Burr had recruited the men and asked for supplies for war to be purchased. That made him part of the overt act.

Hay called William Eaton to the witness stand. Burr objected on grounds that Eaton's testimony had to do with intention to commit treason, not the act of treason itself. He claimed that the prosecution should have to prove the act of treason itself first, knowing that this was going to be difficult. Marshall adjourned to think about it, deciding the next day that the order in which the prosecution presented witnesses did not matter, and General Eaton was allowed to testify.

Eaton described conversations with Burr during the winter of 1805–1806 in which Burr described his plans to attack Mexico and to cause a revolution in the states west of the Allegheny Mountains. But he knew nothing of Burr's activities on Blennerhassett Island or anywhere else in the West. In response to questioning by the defense, however, Eaton admitted that he had agreed to testify only after the Jefferson administration had paid him money he had been angry about not receiving earlier. This definitely lessened the impact of his testimony.

The next witness for the prosecution was Commodore Truxton. He actually turned out to be helpful to the defense. He admitted that Burr had described his projects to him on several occasions, but he insisted that Burr had never said anything about separating any part of the United States. He testified that Burr had said he would lead an invasion of

Mexico if there was war with Spain. If not, he would settle on the Bastrop lands.

Peter Taylor, the Blennerhassetts' gardener, was called on to testify. He described conversations with Blennerhassett about the attack on Mexico and about the gathering of men and supplies on the island in December 1806. Taylor testified that Blennerhassett had told him that "Colonel Burr would be the King of Mexico, and Mrs. Alston, daughter of Colonel Burr, was to be Queen of Mexico, whenever Colonel Burr died."[15]

Another witness for the prosecution was Jacob Allbright, a worker who had been hired by Blennerhassett to help build a kiln for drying corn. He stated that the young men on the island carried rifles and pistols, as was the custom in those days, but there were no bayonets or large quantities of bullets or other military supplies. Allbright had been on Blennerhassett Island on December 10, 1806, when boats were being quickly loaded in an attempt to beat the militia that was headed there. Around midnight, as he remembered it, several of the men were standing around a bonfire when General Tupper of Marietta laid his hands on Blennerhassett and claimed to arrest him. Allbright reported that when seven or eight of the men pointed their muskets at Tupper, he immediately backed off.

Interestingly, General Tupper was sitting in the courtroom but was not called by the prosecution to testify. He had stated in a deposition that he "neither had or pretended to have any authority . . . to arrest anyone," that he had not tried to arrest anyone while on the island, and that he "passed about half an hour" there, talking with Blennerhassett and "the people belonging to the boats." He stated that no guns had been pointed at him, "nor any incivility offered him."[16] In short, the government was not proving an overt act of war.

The Defense Makes a Motion

Eventually the defense made a motion that the court should take no further testimony, asking Marshall to decide if the prosecution had provided enough evidence of the levying of war. The discussion of this motion would last more than a week.

Wickham began the defense's case. He argued that the indictment against Burr was a work of fiction, placing him at the scene of the crime, the act of war, when everyone knew that he was not there on December 10. Allbright's story was suspect since it was not supported by Tupper or anyone else, and according to the Constitution, an overt act needed two witnesses. And as for the act of war itself, suppose Blennerhassett had resisted arrest at the hands of General Tupper. Resisting arrest was a serious offense, but by no means was it treason. Wickham also noted that the prosecution was emphasizing that the men on the island carried guns. He then pointed out that they were preparing to travel west along the Ohio and Mississippi rivers and into the wilderness. Of course such travelers would be armed.

Another defense attorney, Benjamin Botts, pointed out that if indeed a war had been fought on Blennerhassett Island in December 1806, it was a war instigated by the Wood County militia. It was fear of the militia that caused

Blennerhassett and the other men to depart hastily for the West, Botts claimed. Botts wondered how this could lead to a charge of levying war against the United States.

The prosecution's case depended on showing that the gathering of men on Blennerhassett Island was the overt act of levying war required by the Constitution. There were plenty of witnesses to testify that this gathering had taken place. The prosecution argued that it did not matter if Burr was not on the island himself, because he was responsible for the gathering. Wirt gave a speech, "Who is Blennerhassett?" in which he called Burr a serpent who ruined Blennerhassett's life. "In the midst of all this peace," Wirt exclaimed, "this innocence, this tranquillity, this feast of mind . . . the destroyer comes:—he comes to turn his paradise into a hell."[17] Biographer James Parton said that this speech received one of the high honors of nineteenth-century American literature when it was put into school-books in the mid-1800s for students to study and memorize.

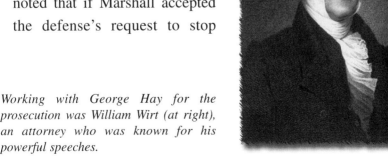

On August 26, George Hay spoke for the prosecution. He noted that if Marshall accepted the defense's request to stop

Working with George Hay for the prosecution was William Wirt (at right), an attorney who was known for his powerful speeches.

taking testimony, it would be taking the trial out of the hands of the jury. In a thinly veiled threat, he stated that this was just the sort of action that had caused Congress to impeach Supreme Court Justice Samuel Chase two years previously.

Burr's lawyer Luther Martin called the supposed conspiracy the "Will o' the Wisp treason" because, "though it is said to be here and there and everywhere, *yet it is nowhere. It exists only in the newspapers and in the mouths of the enemies of the gentleman for whom I appear.*"[18]

He also said, "Permit me . . . to observe that in the case of life and death, where there remains one single doubt in the minds of the jury as to facts, or of the court as to law, it is their duty to decide in favour of life."[19]

Marshall Will Decide

Finally, on Saturday, August 29, the discussion of the motion to stop taking testimony came to an end. Marshall would work through the weekend to prepare a decision. Beginning on Saturday evening, he worked late into the night on Sunday and got up before dawn on Monday to finish. His draft (the longest of his career) ran twenty-five thousand words; it was written in longhand with a quill pen.[20] It would take three hours to read in court.

In it, Marshall said that the only thing wrong with the statement he had made in the *Swartwout-Bollman* case was that it was incomplete. Yes, if there was actually a war levied against the United States,

> if a body of men be actually assembled for the purpose of effecting by force a treasonable purpose, all those who

---

84

perform any part however minute, or however remote from the scene of action . . . are to be considered traitors.[21]

But, he continued,

[the] indictment charges the prisoner with levying war against the United States, and alleges an overt act of levying war. The overt act must be proved . . . by two witnesses. It is not proved by a single witness.[22]

Marshall invited the prosecution to bring forward any evidence it could to prove the overt act of levying war and to prove that Burr was connected to it. The next morning Hay had to report that he had no such evidence. This meant that no more testimony would be heard, and the case would now go to the jury.

Marshall knew that the president would not be happy. In fact, Jefferson had already hinted that Marshall might face an impeachment if he thwarted the president on this. In the closing of his opinion, Marshall stated, "That this Court dare not usurp power is most true. That this Court dare not shrink from its duty is not less true."[23]

Marshall directed the jury to decide a verdict on the charge of treason. "The jury have now heard the opinion of the court on the law of the case. They will apply that law to the facts, and will find a verdict of guilty or not guilty as their own consciences may direct."[24]

The Jury Decides

On Monday, September 1, the jury returned their verdict: "We of the jury say that Aaron Burr is not proved to be

John Randolph, a congressman, was named foreman of the grand jury that convened in Richmond even though he had already formed an opinion regarding Burr's case.

guilty under this indictment by any evidence submitted to us. We therefore find him not guilty."[25]

Burr protested the wording "not proved guilty." Marshall declared the verdict would remain as stated by the jury but would be recorded as a simple "Not Guilty."

With this verdict, the charges of treason against Burr's companions who were also going to be tried in Richmond were then dropped.

Though the jury would not listen to more arguments regarding the charge of treason, the president instructed Hay to get written testimony from all remaining witnesses so that Congress could decide if Marshall had acted appropriately. (Obviously Jefferson did not think he had.)

But Burr was still under indictment for misdemeanor, and that had to be taken care of next. For this Burr was eligible for bail, however, which was set at $5,000 and posted. When the Alstons left to return to their home in South Carolina, Burr moved into the home they had occupied in Richmond. Amazingly, he still spoke of the possibility of renewing some of his plans.

The trial for misdemeanor began on September 9. More than fifty witnesses were called to the stand, but their statements proved only that Burr wished to lead troops into Mexico if the United States and Spain went to war. If there was a war, the Neutrality Act would not be violated, and there would be no crime. On September 15, Hay asked that the case be dropped, but Burr insisted on having a verdict. After a short consultation, the jurors declared Aaron Burr not guilty.

Though Hay and Jefferson had been unable to make charges stick in Kentucky, Mississippi Territory, or now Virginia, they were not yet ready to admit defeat. Hay asked that Burr, Blennerhassett, and John Smith be sent to Chillicothe, Ohio, to be tried there on a charge of treason for acts of war the prosecution said were committed farther west on the Ohio River. For several weeks, Marshall listened to testimony for and against this motion.

Nearly one week of this testimony came from General Wilkinson. He seemed uneasy, and he contradicted himself so often that he sometimes had to ask permission to change or take back his own statements. Hay was forced to write to the president, "My confidence in [Wilkinson] is destroyed."[26] On the streets of Richmond, Andrew Jackson delighted crowds by ridiculing Wilkinson and proclaiming his guilt.

On Tuesday, October 20, Marshall ruled that there was no justification for holding any of the prisoners for additional acts of treason. Burr and Blennerhassett were to appear in Ohio on the misdemeanor charge, but the government was now preoccupied by troubles with Britain and never pursued those charges.

chapter six

SIGNIFICANCE OF THE TRIAL

HISTORICAL IMPACT— The people who came to Richmond for the trial of Aaron Burr had been treated to quite a spectacle. There had been great speeches by some of the best lawyers of the day, sandwiched between long hours of monotonous droning. There had been excited debate on the streets and in the homes and businesses of the city, as well as in the newspapers that carried the debate across the nation. What was it that had ignited the public's intense interest in this case?

Perhaps if we remember that the American nation was only about thirty years old in 1807 and that the Constitution had been in effect for less than twenty years, we can begin to imagine how threatening the alleged conspiracy would seem. The signing of the Declaration of Independence and the battles of the Revolution would be remembered by a significant number of Americans who were alive when those events took place. Indeed, the author of the Declaration of Independence had become president, and the man now accused of treason had been his vice president, had in fact been tied with him for president, and had fought in the Revolution.

At the same time that there were these connections with America's roots, there is the fact that America was changing. There were new states that had never been colonies, and a growing population beyond the Appalachian Mountains that lived very differently from the people on the Atlantic seaboard and faced different problems. There had already been talk of parts of the country splitting off into a new country over a number of issues. Loyalty to a state or region vied with loyalty to country, and the chances of having the young nation torn apart must have seemed very real. Add to this the feeling of vulnerability against the navy of Britain and the army of France, and we can understand the near hysteria that swept the country in response to the conspiracy and the excited atmosphere in which the trial was set.

As for the trial itself, it was referred to at the time, and for at least one hundred years afterward, as "the greatest criminal trial in American history."[1]

Treason Defined

One of the fundamental questions of this trial was the manner in which treason was to be defined. Traditional English common law precedents, the heritage upon which much of American law was and is based, had included very broad and general criteria for treason, including almost any

John Marshall, Chief Justice of the U.S. Supreme Court, presided over the trial of Aaron Burr for treason. Though President Jefferson threatened him with impeachment, he stood firm in doing what he believed was his duty in Burr's case.

action that a king might find offensive. And it included the idea that "in treason all are principals."[2] This would seem to indicate that anyone who participates in any way is just as guilty as anyone else who participates in any way. However, according to Article III, Section 3 of the U.S. Constitution, witnesses to an overt, or public, act were required. Also, the only overt acts of treason allowed by the Constitution were the actual levying of war against the United States or giving aid and comfort to its enemies. What was not completely clear was whether or not the levying of war had to be done in person or whether it could be done at a distance and through other people. By defining treason in a fairly narrow sense, as Marshall did in this case, he limited the ways this charge could be made against enemies of the government.

One of the results of this was to make proof of treason much more difficult—in fact, some would argue, nearly impossible. Prosecutors since then have gotten around this to some extent by using the charge of espionage, or spying. This provides a way to put individuals on trial who have worked undercover against the United States without actually levying war. A related crime of much concern in the early twenty-first century is terrorism. The legal issues surrounding the trials of individuals accused of these crimes are no less complicated than those facing John Marshall in 1807. Modern-day lawyers and judges have often looked to his words to help argue and decide the cases of today.

Separation of Powers

Other extremely important issues raised in the trial dealt with the separation of powers and executive privilege. When Burr requested that a subpoena be issued to Jefferson, requiring him to produce certain papers, an important issue was raised. Did the court have the right to subpoena the president? Each branch of the government—the legislative, judicial, and executive—was carefully separated from the other two by the Constitution. Under what circumstances could one branch tell another what to do?

In those early days of the United States, the answer to this question was not always clear. John Marshall would play an important role in providing an answer that would help make the Constitution a living and effective document. By determining that a subpoena could be issued, Marshall introduced the principle that the president was not above the law. Jefferson, in turn, seemed to have successfully maintained the principle of separation of powers in the way he responded to the subpoena. Even Marshall conceded that "vexatious and unnecessary" subpoenas were not to be issued against the chief executive. Subpoenas became acceptable only when presidential material was "essential to the justice of the case."[3]

It is somewhat ironic that Marshall, a leader of the Federalist party, which had fought for strong central government, found himself standing up for individual liberty against government authority in this case. Conversely, Jefferson, the writer of the Declaration of Independence and leader of the Republicans, who did not favor a great deal of power in the hands of the central government, nevertheless tried to assert governmental power in the form of executive privilege in this case. In any event, when President Richard Nixon tried to claim executive privilege in 1974, the Supreme Court would honor the precedent set by John Marshall—that when the documents in question are essential to justice, even the president of the United States cannot withhold them.

chapter seven

AFTER THE TRIAL

AFTERMATH—In the wake of the trial, both Burr and Blennerhassett faced a mountain of debt. At the end of October 1807, Burr went to Baltimore and then Philadelphia, working with lawyers to stay out of debtors' prison and hiding from mobs that threatened to hang him. Blennerhassett bitterly complained that Burr seemed not to care that the Irishman's home had been destroyed and his fortune was gone. Blennerhassett did receive some money from Joseph Alston when he threatened to make public information about Alston's part in Burr's activities. Then Blennerhassett purchased a cotton farm in Mississippi in hopes of creating a new fortune.

In Search of Friends

In June 1808, Burr left for England. He still hoped to collect funding for some sort of project involving the conquest of Spanish colonies in America.[1] For a short while, he was a welcome guest in a number

Following Burr's trial, Harman Blennerhassett complained to Burr that his home was destroyed and his money gone. The Blennerhassett Mansion, shown above, has been restored and is now a historical site.

of comfortable homes, while he spoke with British government officials. But in April 1809, he was ordered to leave England due to debts he accumulated there and perhaps also due to pressure on the British from Jefferson. From this point on, Burr would spend four long years in Europe, traveling from England to Sweden, Denmark, Germany, and finally, France, trying to regain power and purpose. But none of the European powers were interested in dealing with him, and Burr became increasingly poor and lonely.

Burr's daughter, Theodosia, at home with her husband and son in South Carolina, was often ill during this time. Burr begged her to join him in Europe, where he hoped physicians could cure her of her mysterious maladies. But she never made the trip. They did stay in contact with each other through numerous detailed letters. Theodosia continued to regret that his great plans had come to nothing. "No doubt there are many other roads to happiness," she wrote to him, "but this appeared so perfectly suitable to you."[2] She continued to believe in his greatness and marveled at his ability to endure the difficulties he faced. "You appear to me so superior, so elevated above all other men," she wrote. "I had rather not live than not be the daughter of such a man."[3]

Burr had difficulty securing a passport to return home, at least in part, he believed, due to Jefferson's continued efforts against him. He was low on funds, selling the souvenirs he had bought for his daughter and grandson to get money for food. Finally, he was granted a passport to leave France, and after first being forced to land in Amsterdam, and then England, he finally arrived in Boston on May 4, 1812. Disguised with wig and whiskers, and using the assumed name of Adolphus Arnot, he traveled from Boston to New York after being assured by his old friend Samuel Swartwout that he would not be arrested for his debts.

Just eleven days later, on June 18, a declaration of war was issued in what became known as the War of 1812. This made travel across the Atlantic Ocean even more difficult and dangerous than before and might have kept Burr much longer in Europe had he not returned to the United States when he did.

In July, Burr opened a law office. He was immediately

able to attract many clients, for though he was a social outcast, he was still remembered as an excellent lawyer.

Then came news of the sudden death of his grandson at the end of June. The boy had only recently turned ten. Of course, Burr and the boy's parents were extremely sorrowful.

After several months, it was arranged for the heartbroken and ill Theodosia to travel by sea to New York to be with her father. Travel was dangerous with the United States at war with Britain, but a small fast ship called the *Patriot* was leaving Charleston, South Carolina, for New York, a voyage that could be expected to take five or six days. Burr waited at the dock in New York, but Theodosia was never seen again. There had been a terrible storm along the coast while the ship was at sea, and it is likely that it sank. There were also stories that the passengers may have been murdered by pirates. Pathetically, Burr waited at the harbor for many days, not able to believe that even his beloved Theodosia could be taken from him.

For the rest of his life, Burr was largely looked on with disapproval, being thought of as an ambitious politician, the man who killed Hamilton, and a traitor to his country.

He might have taken some small comfort in the fact that Wilkinson's reputation had suffered as well. Wilkinson died in 1825 and would be remembered as one of America's most disreputable soldiers.

Blennerhassett too had suffered since they had parted ways. His cotton farm in Mississippi did not do well, thanks in part to the War of 1812. In 1819, he moved briefly to Canada. Then in 1822, he returned to his homeland, Ireland,

and then moved to England. He died in 1831, a poor man who had had so much and lost it all. In an effort to provide for her children, Margaret Blennerhassett returned to the United States to seek reimbursement from the government for property that had been taken from her husband because of his association with Burr. She died in New York in 1842 before the government could respond.

Burr lived to the age of eighty. He is remembered as a man whose ambition overshadowed his accomplishments.

Burr lived for many more years, often in debt, or nearly so. Still, he was kind and generous to those who had stood by him, including his former lawyer, Luther Martin, whom he cared for in his home when Martin was poor and ill.

In 1830, Burr suffered the first of several strokes that caused some temporary paralysis. In July 1833, he married Eliza Bowen Jumel. Madame Jumel was the widow of a wine trader and a very wealthy woman. He was seventy-seven. She was fifty-eight. Within months, Burr was ill and would eventually suffer further strokes. Within a year, his wife sued Burr for divorce, most likely, it seems, for mishandling her money. (She was granted a divorce decree; ironically, it took effect the day of Burr's death.)

In his last days, Burr was asked if he had really wanted to separate the West from the United States. He declared that he would have as readily undertaken to invade the moon as to separate the Union. When he learned that Americans had declared the independence of Texas, he is said to have cried, "There! You see? I was right! I was only thirty years too soon! What was treason in me thirty years ago, is patriotism now!"[4]

At the end of his life, Burr was living at the Hotel St. James on Staten Island, near a friend, Judge Ogden Edwards, who looked after him, and this is where he died on September 14, 1836. He was buried with military honors near his father and grandfather at Princeton, New Jersey. The president of the college gave a sermon, and many of the students witnessed the ceremony. Later, a grave marker would indicate that he had been a colonel in the Army of the Revolution and vice president of the United States.

Questions for Discussion

1. Should the president of the United States have to obey all the laws of Congress and the decisions of the Supreme Court?

2. Should the president be forced to turn over documents to a court even if he or she feels they are too sensitive to be made public?

3. If a person has been charged with a crime against the government, such as treason, is he or she still entitled to a fair trial?

4. Should John Marshall have had Thomas Jefferson arrested for not complying in full with the subpoena? Should a court be able to arrest the president?

5. Why were the framers of the U.S. Constitution concerned about defining treason in such narrow terms?

6. Should national security issues ever take greater importance than personal rights in a trial?

7. Have we become too concerned about the rights of the accused at the expense of the rights of society? Do you think the accused have too many rights?

8. Do you think there are times when the president has too much power?

9. Do you think there are times when the Supreme Court has too much power?

10. Should there be limits on what can be printed in newspapers about someone who is on trial?

Chapter Notes

Chapter 1. Prisoner!

1. William H. Safford, *The Life of Harman Blennerhassett* (Chillicothe, Ohio: Ely, Allen & Looker, 1850), p. 146.

2. James Parton, *The Life and Times of Aaron Burr*, vol. II (Boston: Houghton, Osgood & Co., 1881), p. 101.

Chapter 2. Lawyer and Politician

1. Philip Vail, *The Great American Rascal: The Turbulent Life of Aaron Burr* (New York: Hawthorn Books, 1973), p. 66.

2. Donald Barr Chidsey, *The Great Conspiracy: Aaron Burr and His Strange Doings in the West* (New York: Crown Publishers, 1967), p. 35.

3. Vail, p. 107.

Chapter 3. The First Trip West

1. Milton Lomask, *Aaron Burr: The Conspiracy and Years of Exile, 1805–1836* (New York: Farrar, Straus, & Giroux, 1982), p. 58.

2. Margaret L. Coit, *The Life History of the United States: Vol. 3, 1789–1829, The Growing Years* (New York: Time, Inc., 1963), p. 83

3. Lomask, p. 112.

4. Ibid.

5. Walter F. McCaleb, *The Aaron Burr Conspiracy* (New York: Wilson-Erickson, Inc., 1903), p. 69.

Chapter 4. The Burr War

1. Milton Lomask, *Aaron Burr: The Conspiracy and*

Years of Exile, 1805–1836 (New York: Farrar, Straus, & Giroux, 1982), p. 136.

2. Ibid.

3. Henry S. Randall, *The Life of Thomas Jefferson*, vol. III (New York: Derby & Jackson, 1858), p. 183.

4. Walter F. McCaleb, *The Aaron Burr Conspiracy* (New York: Wilson-Erickson, Inc., 1903), p. 109.

5. James Parton, *The Life and Times of Aaron Burr*, vol. II (Boston: Houghton, Osgood & Co., 1881), p. 82.

6. McCaleb, p. 140.

7. William H. Safford, *The Life of Harman Blennerhassett* (Chillicothe, Ohio: Ely, Allen & Looker, 1850), p. 98.

8. McCaleb, p. 169.

9. Lomask, p. 186.

10. Ibid., p. 195.

11. McCaleb, p. 238.

12. Buckner F. Melton, Jr., *Aaron Burr: Conspiracy to Treason* (New York: John Wiley & Sons, 2002), p. 151.

13. Roger G. Kennedy, *Burr, Hamilton, and Jefferson: A Study in Character* (New York: Oxford University Press, 2000), p. 140.

14. Jean Edward Smith, *John Marshall: Definer of a Nation* (New York: Henry Holt and Company, 1996), p. 354.

15. Melton, p. 156.

16. Lomask, p. 217.

17. Safford, p. 125.

18. Jonathan Daniels, *Ordeal of Ambition* (Garden City, N.Y.: Doubleday and Co., 1970), p. 355.

Chapter 5. The Trial

1. James Parton, *The Life and Times of Aaron Burr*, vol. II (Boston: Houghton, Osgood & Co., 1881), p. 108.

2. Milton Lomask, *Aaron Burr: The Conspiracy and*

Years of Exile, 1805–1836 (New York: Farrar, Straus, & Giroux, 1982), p. 229.

3. Henry S. Randall, *The Life of Thomas Jefferson*, vol. III (New York: Derby & Jackson, 1858), p. 208.

4. Parton, p. 118.

5. Pierre M. Irving, *Life and Letters of Washington Irving*, vol. 1 (New York: G.P. Putnam, 1863), p. 202.

6. Randall, p. 206.

7. Ibid., p. 211.

8. Jonathan Daniels, *Ordeal of Ambition* (Garden City, N.Y.: Doubleday and Co., 1970), p. 364.

9. Buckner F. Melton, Jr., *Aaron Burr: Conspiracy to Treason* (New York: John Wiley & Sons, 2002), p. 185.

10. Thomas Perkins Abernethy, *The Burr Conspiracy* (New York: Oxford University Press, 1954), pp. 239–240.

11. Melton, p. 189.

12. Edward S. Corwin, *John Marshall and the Constitution, A Chronicle of the Supreme Court* (New Haven, Conn.: Yale University Press, 1919), p. 99.

13. Lomask, p. 261.

14. Walter F. McCaleb, *The Aaron Burr Conspiracy* (New York: Wilson-Erickson, Inc., 1903), p. 283.

15. Ibid., p. 81.

16. Lomask, p. 267.

17. William H. Safford, *The Life of Harman Blennerhassett* (Chillicothe, Ohio: Ely, Allen & Looker, 1850), p. 68.

18. Lomask, p. 277.

19. Ibid., p. 278.

20. Jean Edward Smith, *John Marshall: Definer of a Nation* (New York: Henry Holt and Company, 1996), p. 370.

21. Corwin, p. 108.

22. Smith, p. 371.

23. Corwin, p. 112.

24. Abernethy, p. 247.

25. Melton, p. 216.

26. Corwin, p. 114.

Chapter 6. Significance of the Trial

1. Edward S. Corwin, *John Marshall and the Constitution, A Chronicle of the Supreme Court* (New Haven, Conn.: Yale University Press, 1919), p. 86.

2. Ibid., p. 104.

3. William F. Swindler, *The Constitution and Chief Justice Marshall* (New York: Dodd, Mead and Co., 1978), pp. 43–44.

Chapter 7. After the Trial

1. Walter F. McCaleb, *The Aaron Burr Conspiracy* (New York: Wilson-Erickson, Inc., 1903), p. 301.

2. James Parton, *The Life and Times of Aaron Burr*, vol. II (Boston: Houghton, Osgood & Co., 1881), p. 165.

3. Ibid., p. 188.

4. Jonathan Daniels, *Ordeal of Ambition* (Garden City, N.Y.: Doubleday and Co., 1970), p. 421.

Glossary

circuit court—A lower court in the judicial system. In Burr's day, these lower courts often held sessions in different places, and judges traveled from place to place, which was called "riding the circuit."

common law—Law based on custom or tradition.

conspiracy—A plan among a group of people to work together on an illegal activity.

district attorney—A lawyer for the government or the people of a certain area.

due process—Basic protections guaranteed to a person accused of a crime.

executive privilege—Certain rights of the head of the executive branch of government.

grand jury—A group assigned to decide if there is enough evidence to formally accuse an individual of a crime.

habeas corpus—A legal order preventing people from being held in jail without sufficient reason. According to the Constitution, habeas corpus cannot be denied except in cases of rebellion or when public safety requires it.

indictment—The formal written statement charging someone with a crime.

levy war—To carry out war.

misdemeanor—A crime that is not as serious as a felony.

national security—Things that affect the safety and well-being of the nation as a whole.

overt act—A visible or open action.

precedent—A legal decision that can be followed in later cases.

subpoena—An order from the court to be a witness or produce evidence at a trial.

treason—According to the U.S. Constitution, the actual levying of war against the United States.

Further Reading

Books

Blumberg, Rhoda. *What's the Deal? Jefferson, Napoleon, and the Louisiana Purchase.* Washington, D.C.: National Geographic Society, 1998.

Collier, Christopher, and James Lincoln Collier. *The Jeffersonian Republicans: The Louisiana Purchase and the War of 1812, 1800–1823.* New York: Benchmark Books, 1999.

Corrick, James A. *The Louisiana Purchase.* San Diego: Lucent Books, 2001.

Ingram, Scott. *Aaron Burr and the Young Nation.* Farmington Hills, Mich.: Gale Group, 2002.

Whitelaw, Nancy. *More Perfect Union: The Story of Alexander Hamilton.* Greensboro, N.C.: Reynolds, Morgan, 1997.

Internet Addresses

The Treason Trial of Aaron Burr
<http://www.law.umkc.edu/faculty/projects/ftrials/burr/burraccount.html>

The American Presidency
<http://gi.grolier.com/presidents/ea/vp/vpburr.html>

The Duel
<http://www.pbs.org/wgbh/amex/duel/sfeature/burrconspiracy.html>

Index